VOLUME 92 OF THE YALE SERIES OF YOUNGER POETS

# My Shining Archipelago

Talvikki Ansel

FOREWORD BY JAMES DICKEY

Yale University Press
New Haven and London

Published with the assistance of a
grant to honor James Merrill.

Designed by James J. Johnson
and set in Kennerley Medium
type by Tseng Information
Systems, Inc., Durham,
North Carolina.

Printed in the United States of
America by Thomson-Shore, Inc.,
Dexter, Michigan.

Library of Congress
Cataloging-in-Publication Data

Ansel, Talvikki, 1962–
My shining archipelago /
Talvikki Ansel ; foreword by
James Dickey.
p. cm. — (Yale series of younger
poets ; v. 92)
ISBN 0-300-07031-4 (alk. paper).
— ISBN 0-300-07032-2 (pbk. :
alk. paper)
1. Amazon River Region—
Poetry. I. Title. II. Series.
PS3551.N69M9   1997
811'.54—dc21        96-45321

A catalogue record for this book
is available from the British
Library.

The paper in this book meets
the guidelines for permanence
and durability of the Committee
on Production Guidelines for
Book Longevity of the Council
on Library Resources.

10  9  8  7  6  5  4  3  2  1

# Contents

# Acknowledgments

Grateful acknowledgment is made to the publications in which the following poems first appeared:

*Hayden's Ferry Review*: "From Stone"

*The Iowa Review*: "Filaments," "Fishing"

*The Journal*: "My Shining Archipelago," "Stories: Wolf Children"

*The Missouri Review*: "In Fragments, In Streams," "Afterwards: Caliban"

*Poetry East*: "Conversation with the Sun Bittern," "Flemish Beauty"

*Shenandoah*: "John Clare"

*Willow Springs*: "You Don't Know What Happened When You Froze"

Sincere gratitude to all who provided encouragement, and to David Wojahn for his generous attention to this manuscript.

# Foreword

When Mallarmé, according to Symbolist doctrine, says that the poet should not describe trees but convey the "horror of the forest," we might also remember that, though poetry has dealt with a great many forests, it has ventured into only a few jungles. Considering the surplus of plant and animal life offered, the sheer exotica, this may at first seem curious, but when considered at more length it is not as odd as it may seem. Though poets, especially romantic poets, like to be overwhelmed by nature, true jungles, such as those through which the Amazon and Orinoco run, are so overwhelming as to dumbfound, or almost. Step from a temperate zone into the endless greenhouse of a rain forest, and consciousness founders, groping to find ways to speak that may be adequate. The horror of the forest is not to be delivered by Symbolist implication but by present and proliferating Fact. All is intensity, as though in such hothouse breathlessness things exist for the express purpose of *being* intense. All colors are collision colors: a single stripe on the wing of a butterfly is painful; one turns away. Brown, ordinarily mild, here strikes the eye like a new concept of brown, conceived and fulfilled at the same time by an unknowable power. An everyday writer will very likely recoil, and turn the movement into a retreat, not able to sustain by words what she has ventured.

But if the writer is as good as Talvikki Ansel, she does sustain it. Ansel finds her way of bringing into language the hellish magnificence, the perverse pluralism, the never-failing imagination based on burning and burning out, death already quivering with rebirth, and behind that, death and rebirth again. More, always more, in the Amazon basin, as though God were helpless in this overconcentrated excess and created by necessity or compulsion: that, here, reality is *compelled* to be thus.

Ansel understands these things because she not only has lived them but continues to do so with a self-passion that matches the orchid, the piranha, the *fer de lance*; her hammock is still strung in the Matto Grosso. There, a primal fear like no other envelops everything, includes everything, and brings in more.

Present always is the sense of expectancy, of something inexplicable and terrible about to happen, as various poisons refine in plants and the heads of serpents, the spider affixes another filament of itself to the huge web where the tarantula struggles, the dread clicking sound of billions of tiny razor jaws comes gradually to be heard: red hunger of the soldier ant multiplied beyond reason, unstoppable lava flow of insects, *La Marabunta*, stripping to skeletons all trees and animals on a fifty-mile front. In the saw-edged shadows of the sun, in the green night of her hammock, Ansel finds her own fraught calm:

> A happiness complete as belief,
> suspended mid-air, the nest in the leaf.

Ansel's ambitious sequence in freewheeling sonnets, "Afterwards: Caliban," is further evidence of the vividness and tenaciousness of her mind, which makes good use of theme and variations. By her particular means, Caliban moves from the island of Prospero to Elizabethan London. The sea comes into things, and the poet writes of it with innocent and charming eloquence:

> The sea's Mercurial flush, endless dove grey,
> The sky like water, but of Other
> Colors: lavender to sand-yellow
> Like the Tortoise glides in the billows
> On Armored wings.

Into London, where "they" have transported him, Caliban bears the subtropical island and its magic, his primitive and monstrous intuitions. Horses

> have smooth, knocking beach-stone hooves,
> Are made to pull carriages, carry wood
> Across London's dull paths.
> Ears like the hare
> They speak a Soft Language. Sweet Breathers:
> They exist solely on the Insubstantial

Grass, dusty Grains. The head is small—the size
Of an owl, a keg.

England and the spellbound tropics mix. Enchantment gets into
food—Caliban is at one point a cook—into topiary shapes alive
and strange as real beasts, into laundry, garbage, jewels of women
and beards of men, streets, bedchambers. Shocked, like Words-
worth at Bartholomew Fair, but avid with "Alchemic Under-
standing," Caliban enters in:

> Watching
> Alone from a casement window the moon
> Casts my lumped, ugly Shadow. Torch flames
> Like salamanders, like the red Silk
> In Cloaks. No, I never found Another
> Like me.

This figure of the poet, misshapen and spellbinding, seems
to me superb. Ansel can stop you dead—and alive—with an ob-
servation, an insight, a metaphor, a word from left field or the
empty sky, the true Mallarméan *azur*. Such astonishments could
not be discovered or given were it not for the daring conjunction
she puts things into: an inspired monster, a subtropical island,
earth-magic and a London once dull, now not.

I don't know whether Ansel would agree, but there may
be three poets here combined in one vision, one attitude: Ansel,
Caliban, and Shelley. If this last surprises, it should be understood
that when the first two of these say that "What I tell you, what
I tell you—/ It is so much smaller than what I can not tell you"
they are saying the same thing as Shelley in his *Defense of Poetry*:
"The most glorious poetry that has ever been communicated to
the world is probably a feeble shadow of the original concep-
tions of the poet." This is noble but dangerous, and I am glad that
neither Caliban nor Ansel believes it, for I do not. The poet is
delivered in and by means of words and only words, and true
poets like Ansel know this without words. Her point of view, her

angles of sight and insight, are all related to verbal exploration, adventure, discovery. If at times her poems seem to wander it is a right wandering: such is her appeal, her daring and stealth, that one follows where she leads, stalking, closing in, going forward, with Caliban lurching and transforming, the chachalaca slung at his waist.

JAMES DICKEY

# One

✹ ✹ ✹

# Study Skins

Grit of cornmeal, borax,
the neck droops over my hand,
limp wings. Clean slit
from the cloaca, I peel back
skin from the breast—gently
not to stretch it. How neatly
it all fits together. Flies.
Outside, a blackbird squawks.
                    Rough bumps
of the feather tracts under skin,
each feather a bump. The innards
textbook perfect: gleaming
liver lobes, the heart
clean as a thumb, trachea—
windpipe—fluted hollow
holding the breath. Inside out
the wing's white bone
juts up, the thigh.
My hair falls into my face—so easy
to dig out the skull,
pry out the eyes. Outside,
the air all brightness, warm bayberry:
light, whole and beating. I think
what's to keep
me from dissipating, evaporating,
like a breath
or the blackbird's call?
I make a body from a stick
wrapped in cotton, imbed
it in the skull. My hands
sticky and caught
with pieces of tissue and down,
some in my hair, on my brow.
When I'm done, the guts
a small pile on the newspaper,

the birds, wings folded,
stare straight up to the ceiling.
Eyes filled with cotton,

wide and blank as if
they've seen some mystery
I don't see, whole—*fluted*—
which means furrowed, clear.

# Flemish Beauty

Yesterday, all winter,
I had not thought of pears, considered:
*pear*. The tear-shaped, papery core,
precise seeds. This one channelled
through with worm tunnels.
Bruises, a rotten half—
sometimes there's nothing left
to drop into the pot.

                        That phrase
I could have said: "you still
have us . . ."
               The knife
slides easily beneath the skins,
top to base, spiralling
them away.

The insubstantial us.
It could as well be the pear
talking to the river, turning to
the grass ("you still have us").
Besides, it's just *me*
a pear in my hand (the slop bucket full
of peels) — and sometimes, yes, that
seems enough: a pear—

                       this larger one,
yellow-green, turning to red:
"Duchess" maybe, "Devoe,"
or what I want to call it: "Flemish
Beauty."
            When I can't sleep,
I'll hold my hand as if I held
a pear, my fingers mimicking
the curve. The same curve

as the newel post
I've used for years, swinging
myself up to the landing, always
throwing my weight back. And always
nails loosening, mid-bound.

# You Don't Know What Happened
# When You Froze

When buck fever struck,
you stood stiff, unable
to pull the trigger while the herd
crashed past you and
into the woods.

Your cousins—who, one night
when you were all boys, scared
you in the pine grove with a candle
in a cow skull—carried
you to a clearing; they loosened
your hunting vest,
gave you a flask of Jack Daniel's,
and you remembered nothing.

※　※　※

Last night you dreamt of a room—
a room full of fish,
and a swimming pool
where you waded knee-deep
and hauled them all in

except for one, already dead,
a large bluefish wedged
into a corner, its back stiff.

You remember it later: its eye
like a button,
a button on another person's coat.

# Eating

They fed us soft-boiled eggs, six
in a basket covered in a dishcloth. Our mother
with one swift crunch could slice off the tops.
Ralston, grits, cornmeal mush; steel-cut
oats, cooked for a night on the back
of the stove; split-pea soup, heaving
and gumming in the iron pot; cole slaw:

cabbage shredded, peppered and tossed
in mayonnaise; and someone in the kitchen
gnawing on the cabbage stub (for years
I thought it was "costs low"); cod and potatoes,
the fishy-smelling box with the sliding lid
that we all wanted, and the cod soaking
in a bowl, a chunk of dirty snow; the pot
of minestrone our father dropped

coming into the dining room, spectacular,
noodles everywhere, the dog ecstatic, and us
staring down at our placemats not
daring to laugh. And kale, kale
that stayed green and bitter until November,
leaves frosty when we snapped them from
the woody stems. Our mother splitting pods
of cardamom on Sundays and baking
pülla; rowing with our father to an

island where we waded in the chill salt,
pried mussels and periwinkles
from dark rocks, and steamed them in weeds
on a smoking driftwood fire, but that
was long ago, when we crouched
on the beach, sharpening rose twigs
and digging out the meat.

# Three Ducks

She won't look
when the boys kill the ducks
until her cousin twirls
the drake's head, left, right,
left, right, a head
without a body. This is her mother's
country. The rustle
in the reindeer moss was a lizard
coming out to sun.
There are more flowers here
than anywhere else. Forget-me-nots
are sky blue, baby blue,
like a scorpion's tail
they curl around her finger.
She is sorry
for the ants she's killed.
The wagtail that nests
under the porch is territorial.
She shot a .22 once, hit
the target her brothers couldn't.
The electric fence is smooth,
then the sting. They quacked
when she brought them soaked
breadcrumbs every morning.
Her brother is sixteen
and won't swim naked
with them anymore. Her mother
reads to them from
*The Wizard of Oz*, there's a cupboard
of human heads, jabbering,
a pot of meat glue.
At night it is light.
Dragonflies perch
on her bare shoulders. She hates
her mother and brother

when they laugh at her. On the cliff
are two pines, one
has a branch around the other.
She hides from everyone
on the outhouse roof,
watches the path
and the orange-barked trees.

# Conversation with the
# Sun Bittern

It preens on a root at the edge of the *igarapo*.
Light lights its lower mandible and brick-red eye.

I say, "why am I talking to you?"
"I don't know," it says, and spears a snail. Its head
is striped, its back mottled.

I tell it about the drawer with the false bottom in
my mother's desk.

I tell it about the letter I haven't finished, to a
person who gave me some diamonds.

"I know all that," it says, and watches a minnow in among
the mangrove roots.

"You know what you must do," it says, "you must stop . . ."
"Breeding miniature horses," I say.
"They are useless," it says.

I watch it lift one foot, and then the other. A drop
of water glistens on the tip of its bill.
"I know," I say, "but sometimes I am afraid."

# Filaments

The woman pushes away
from the microscope, she would rather
be somewhere else. Water
collected in the gutter below
the window is sparkling.
Under the lenses, Volvox aureus
somersaults and splits,
sends its green colonies
rolling out, to split
and roll. She has read, "Volvox
is like a universe
of individual stars, fixed
in an invisible firmament." She thinks
there are Volvox in the gutter,
in China
where her brother is. Today
in a store she saw a tiny wooden
bug in a sandalwood nut; its legs
hung loose, trembled
with the movement from little weights
attached. She hopes he is all right,
her brother. Seventy
years ago her grandmother, Ardith
Thrift, leaned over the puzzle
her father was carving; said, "I want
to make it beautiful" when
her mother asked her
what kind of dress
she would make from the cotton
brought into the swamp. The swamp
where everything is green, Volvox
dividing; rolling off
the alligator's lip, through
the cooter's belly, into Red's
water dish. And everything

not in water is coming
out of water: the trees rising,
the hummock
where Ardith lived; the stand
of cypress, where there was still
an ivory bill, even the sky
at night—darkness
out of darkness, studded
with stars—which the granddaughter
now follows in constellations:

                           the arc

to Arcturus; Big Dipper
to Polaris, the celestial pole.

# Fishing

The beach rocks when he drops me off
     in the morning—and the lawn
and my bed, when I sleep after fishing
     all night. My chest
and stomach flat on the mattress,
     rise and fall, like a line
on the fathometer's spool of turning
     paper. My eyelids—I close
my eyes and see the red glow
     of the compass in the cabin.
When I wake, everything will be still:
     my boots at the door, the lawn
fresh with light, upright cedars,
     horizontal stretch of sea.

※ ※ ※

In the cabin we drink coffee, pale hands
     cupped around mugs, below us the net
tears into mud. When the winter
     flounder leave, the window panes
come into the bay. Their grey backs
     speckled with color, bodies
so thin I can see bones through
     skin. I pick through them
with a nail on the end of a stick,
     save the largest, shovel the rest
back over the side. Some have been pressed
     against the mesh of the net, flesh
like a child's palm, bruised and soft.

※ ※ ※

I have tried so many times to take
     this photograph: white door frame,

view beyond: green strip of lawn,
       sea wall, clouds above breakers,
but I can never focus the inside
       and the outside, the kitchen
darkens and the cedars blur. Ink flushes
       onto my hands when I cut the squid
into squares; it comes clean in water.
       On days when I do not fish
I walk the island. In a sumac bush,
       a mockingbird flutters like a scrap
of torn curtain.

❊   ❊   ❊

When I was a child, they would bring up
       eels from the river by the house:
buckets full—they did not begin or end,
       twisting around themselves in a circle
continuous and winding; I still think
       some morning I will wake up
and everything will be clear to me:
       squares of light on the ceiling,
the wallpaper, the curtains in dotted
       swiss, and I will say, "this
is my life." The knotted fringe stilled
       in the breeze.

# Two

❋ ❋ ❋

# In Fragments, In Streams

### i

The *Teatro Amazonas*, remnant
from the rubber barons, who sent
their laundry to France. Turn of the century
embroidered hanky in this city—
scrape in the jungle, once embellished:
the opera house, a fish market designed
by Alexandre Eiffel, dark and cool.
Inside, the piranhas and pirarucu
smooth and twitching on the marble counters.
Outside in the bright heat, the vendors
hawking watches, the radios and stereos,
and always the *Teatro*, calm as cream. Stone
from Italy, and plush seat covers within,
a painted ceiling, once—Jenny Lind.

### ii

Somewhere the doctor who cured the sores
on my leg, iodine, bright purple swab;
a hummingbird drinking from a stream—
*Thalurania furcata*,
I can't remember what reserve or day,
only a violet breast, the throat, green.
Memory wholly concentrated in
a scatter of images: dubbed movie, the screen,
dull glow of the streets from the river,
an intensification, bright finch for sale.
My identification card, the woman
putting all her weight on my thumb: photo-
graph, name, date of birth, title—all in ink—
"Biologista," my finger, indelible print.

### iii

A language I never knew well, calling
a street a star, or *bathing waking*.
A confusion of pavement, cabbies running
red lights, and one road out to the forest—
where my name became "Talvez," which meant
*maybe* in Portuguese. I knew a few
words: belly, meat, rice, beans; evenings
spent in my hammock, the *mateiros'* low
indecipherable speech, sharp slap
of dominoes. A sound in the distance
low and rushing, rain in the canopy.
Bird with a whistle like a piccolo,
dripping and ageless, and all of us
in Latin, Brazilian-tinged: *Cyphorinus.*

### iv

At night, coolness like water lapping
around our hammocks, wrapped in a woolen
blanket, I'd rock, listen for the laughing-
frogs, the potoo's "poor-me-all-alone,"
one foot pushing off from the ground. I
never expected this: a bird's small, pale
eggs in a laced-up palm frond, how easily
trees would fall, tilting up from the fine earth,
coming down with a tangle of vines.
Afloat in the green island of forest,
slipping into the stream each evening
minnows would nudge my shoulders and spine.
A happiness as complete as belief,
suspended midair, the nest in the leaf.

**v**

There is no one to tell this to now; how,
after, I knew the difference between light
and sunlight when I left Brazil, the frogs
like bright jewels after a rain. To the right
of the path by the stream a coral snake
like a tender, beaded thread; the balance
of familiarity and awe. Sometimes
now at night, I close my eyes and can hear
silence and then the piha's piercing cry.
I still keep a cake of Phebo soap hidden
in a drawer, a corroded watch, slides
that are overexposed, washed-out from sun,
an occasional luminous photograph
in fog. But clearings, the sky white, earth black.


**vi**

Halley's Comet crossed the jungle sky
that April, six mornings in a row
I woke to hike out to a clearing
and never saw it. Somewhere above the low
clouds, the constellations: *Cruzeiro do
sul*, all wings and tail like a giant
macaw. Dust and rain puddles. Who knows
what comes before, or trails after;
my first night in the city, a sloth
on the headboard, my sudden fear: *what have I
done this time?* A bat in the net at dawn,
leaf nosed, the ancient face familiar,
inscrutable, like the eroded trail,
the mute sloth's remnant stub of tail.

## vii

Before first light, we would open the nets
for birds and wait, half dozing on a log,
slapping tapir-flies, pulling out
their tongues. A number for each bird, a dog-
eared field guide, a scale, and a ruler
for measuring wings. They hung upside down
until we took them out: first feet, then shoulders
and head, an aluminum band around
one leg: the *Galbulas'*, soft and yellow,
hummingbirds' too short for bands, the heart's
flicker in the palm of your hand. To know
their names: antbird, antshrike, *Myrmetherula*,
wren. Familiar plumage, song—it stirs—
flies, and I can't follow where it has gone.

## viii

Rainy season, and the days fading
in and out of showers. Sound in the trees
just before the downpour, eyes stinging,
a rivulet down the small of my back.
We'd stand under the ground palms, or lean, head bowed
against a tree trunk's buttresses. Water.
Once, a sound like quiet frogs, but instead,
a lek of brown hummingbirds: six, perched
and hovering, flicking their tails. So quick
they become not blur, but "tink, tink,"
sound in motion. Once I woke and a flock
of trumpeters was foraging on the ground
around me, their plumage velvety clean.
In the rain, washing my socks in the stream.

## ix

Burrowing into the pages of *War
and Peace* at night, in the circle
of my headlamp: Natasha, the fragrant samovar,
and a fat-toed gecko all illumin-
ated. Sitting above a valley, I watched
it fill with light, green and green, each leaf turn
in the breeze: I can hardly remember
the voices of friends, it becomes harder
to write letters. Ripe *maracuja*, tart
and sweet. A royal flycatcher, its crest
like a crown imperial-lily: rust,
tipped with blue, rising and setting. In
the distance, the howler monkeys' soft roar,
each night, clouds, and I don't want anything more.


## x

I sleep and wake, sleep, rock suspended in
the dark, hammock snug along the length
of my spine. An owl calls, the bliss of two
more hours of sleep, a sea of forest
around the camp. I was only afraid
a few times; walking alone down a road,
a man with a gun, a dead bird, heading
towards me, then gone. When a poacher stole
our cheese, I woke at every branch snap,
sweating. Reassuring, the stars,
silhouettes of trees, spiders' webs
in the morning, filaments strung from
branch to branch—the old balm, a silken ball
on a wound; the second owls' answering call.

## xi

To catch the truck to Manaus, we hike out
of the forest, cross a cleared hectare, and I,
ashamed to find the open space relief.
Knee-high grass, too bright to photograph.
My face burning in the sun, the sky rolls in
on itself. We step over charred, dead trees.
On stumps, termite mounds like growths. A few pale
cattle watch us from a rise, ghost ships,
in the heat, the herd appears to quiver.
In town, it's too hot to sleep. The mosquitos
burst when I slap them on my legs. Luxury—
electric shower head, in the flow
I lift my arms to turn off the hot,
like a slap, the humiliating shock.

## xii

The Rio Negro meets the Amazon,
black against brown river, they run along
like the horizon line, dark trees and sky
undisturbed. At the waterfront the black
vultures squabble like chickens, boats bring in
bananas, *arroz,* and *farinha,*
on the *rua,* someone has a monkey
on a leash. I eat too much, feel
clumsy. When the shopkeepers speak to me,
I misunderstand them, their cruzeiros;
later, a pack on my back, another
slung against my chest, I slip off the log
bridges, there's nowhere I seem to belong,
the toucans' even "yip-yap" at dawn.

## xiii

In the camp, the leaf-cutter ants defol-
iate a tree, piece by piece they carry
the green squares into the ground. Ozmundo
the *mateiro*'s left eye is cloudy,
he brings three chickens to the camp, their crows
confuse me at dawn. A BBC crew
comes out, I don't want to see them; below
my hammock: my boots, socks, shirt, pants
and headlamp, I dress as I wake. I don't
want their *cerveja*, fresh fruit, jokes
about the instability of hammocks, they
hardly notice me anyway. Eating
last night's cold rice that morning, an ant
clung to the underside of my tongue.

## xiv

Along the road, the bright painted crosses
on the steepest banks, overturned buses,
people waiting in the rain. A deep
gouge with smaller rivers running down it,
mud slick as ice, and driving we slide
sideways. My last day in the forest
I tilt my head back in the stream, the palms
silhouetted against the sky, under
my butt the water hollows out sand;
why did I come here? Everything slips
away. On the road, the man with a gun,
a dead chachalaca slung at his waist;
back in the city, rain clouds stud
the grey sky, my clothes are reddened with mud.

### xv

An agouti runs into the patched sun-
light beneath the trees, I want a single
word for forest, the *oropendula*'s
green-bottle bubble call as it spills and climbs
on the branch tips. My journal
is in the bottom of my pack, I can't
imagine not being here. In between net runs
I eat crackers, shave off a wart
on my index finger with the blade
of my knife. On a twig, a kingfisher
the size of a sparrow blinks and flicks
its tail. It is Thanksgiving; I want
to touch it, but it flies, to a farther tree
and I walk on, precariously.

### xvi

In the airport when I left, a scissor-
tailed flycatcher way above, between
the glass dome and grey sky. Everything in
bits and pieces now, the glass of the plane
against my forehead, below the river
silver among thick trees. The come and go
of images, a dove filling my hand.
I wouldn't know how to even find
the road, it is so far from me now. In a Chicago
museum one winter, a *Morpho* butterfly,
faded past fading, pinned flat behind
glass would only mean a dull homesickness,
and nothing to the crowd, pressing around;
sliver-thin image, metallic-blueness drowned.

### xvii

I was walking the edge of the forest
once, a little lost but not too lost,
looking for the path in. It was evening
and foggy. On my left, the trees—a great
wave of grey in the fog; the strands of barbed
wire to stop the cows were balancing
drops of water, and every hair on my arm
was white with fog. I have never told
anyone this. How, seeing it all I thought
I wouldn't have cared if I were dying.
A pearl kite hawking insects, brilliant
tangled beetle in the net—and I think I
could have walked forever into the trees,
into the breaking trees.

### xviii

Waking, months after I leave the jungle,
I have lost something in sleep; I curl
under my blankets. My toes numb,
I push a foot against the wall until
I rock slightly in my bed. New England
spring, the crocuses bloom and freeze. Brazil
is like a bird in watercolor I thought
I saw a long time ago, a fading ceiling;
I try to remember one thing, a blue
winged moth, sun filtering through the trees,
the spiders spinning their threads across
the paths; when I wake again I am
freezing, and my remembering,
the web I walk through every morning.

# Three

❋ ❋ ❋

# From Stone

Coming into an empty room I find
you crying, you want
the green chair, the chair
you remember being born on. What
can I do to console you?
I would do anything for you. Today

I thought of Senefelder
discovering lithography:
the door open
to the cobbled yard, the laundress
sticks in her head, asks
for a list; he scribbles
on a piece of limestone: two shirts
three trousers, a waistcoat and hose—

why should the swish
of water on a flat rock,
a leather roller matted with ink
express anything I feel now?
Untouching, four birds
on a neighbor's chimney—

autumn: an overcast sky,
from the bluff only the sound
of waves on sand;
a distant pole, a bird, a swallow
wrapped around its heart.

In the 16th century,
it was thought that swallows
spent winters in the bottoms
of lakes. Who wouldn't
reach for that? Solace
of blood and feathers, ensconced
in clay.

# Voyage

On board you fashioned me a clever
workbasket—scrimshaw clothespins,
a spool with our ship sailing
along the rim above the coiled thread,
a pie crimper shaped like a horse-
fish, for me to run
along the edges of the pies.

In all our innocence, we prepared
for this—scurvy, the disease when the skin
stays pinched. Five barrels
of pickled limes, and precautions
from my father the doctor.

Five months into the voyage
I would lose my two white chickens
off the Cape of Good Hope,
and within a year, you
from the rigging. First the cart-
wheel spinning . . .

# John Clare

Spondee; name —
damp earth and distance. This
is what it's like to leave — first
the dirt, robin perched
on the handle of the spade; Mary, up-
ending a bucket for him to sit
while she hisses the milk into a pail,
ear pressed to a flank, lap,
the fern owl's nest. Enclosure, 1810 —
the first act, the moors
all cut like quilt nap. Blue
thread of pain. — Why does *anyone*
think they can step back? (me,
when I close my eyes I
can see the hill beyond
the larch, cows like specks —)
Homesick? Blue flax, birds's eggs,
he writes: the moor, "its only
bondage the circling sky." The blackbird
in the coppice churrs, "we have no name for
burst of spring." Doctor Allen
feels the perfect dome, ellipse —
*ellipsis* — of his skull; phrenology at Fairmead
House for the Insane; vicissitudes of weather on
the subject's mind. *The Flitting*, "summer
like a stranger comes . . . I envy birds,"
sweeping clear sky. John Clare,
"my life hath been one love," escapes:
wet ditches, Mary, "my life
hath been one chain of contradictions,"
in search of Mary — dead now
three years, eating grass.
And this: when he dies the villagers lift
the lid of the coffin, see if it's

he, keep midnight vigil; keep
at bay a London surgeon wanting
to slice the top of his skull, to study
the tempest settling.

# Inscrutable Pig

Round-bellied, straight-flying
birds, the robins settle
for night. I was waiting for owls—bird
whose name has barely changed
from Anglo-Saxon ("they name themselves").
On the hill an inscrutable stone pig
stared out from someone's yard, from
half-closed eyes, balanced in the moss
on its four feet, surprisingly
delicate. When I was eight I wanted
a stone lion. I'm still not sure why.
All afternoon in the *Exeter*
*Book Riddles* and I see how the world
is illuminated in the unravelling,
the altering and renaming. The sea
is *the swan's riding place,*
*the ship's road, the whale's path.*
A sail, *a sea garment.* Waiting
for the soft sloping shoulders
of an owl, I flattened myself against
a sweet gum tree. *Life's house:*
the body. I don't actually remember
deciding to go out, the dusk air
a shadow in the pig's ear;
the riddles end with: say what my
name is. I heard a faint call
from the pines, or maybe imagined it.

# The Periodic Table

On the lake's mercurial surface, waterboatmen's feet
dimple between rain and water, one element.

See, each day falls into itself, this moment
a mole digging in the sod, in its element.

Chart placemats on the table we ate eggs
off latitude and longitude, navigation's precise elements.

Duco cement in my brother's treasure box, fishing
lures, geodes and other mysterious elements.

Rhodesian ridgeback, Rhode Island Red, Rhododendron,
*Rhodium*—who's ever heard of that?

Needless words omitted, gold asters in a vase,
top button unbuttoned, *The Elements of Style*.

One grandfather an admiral, the other an opium addict,
chemist, silversmith—one's ancestral elements.

In the sand by the foundry door, a running dog, lopsided
man, lead heart—cast-off dribbles of an element.

✳  ✳  ✳

An ordinary piece of glassware, or pot
will provide a plant with a lifetime's trace elements.

They've put Iron next to Manganese, assigned it #26.
Don't they know it wants to be with Copper, two over?

"Sn," Tin. Tin snips, handle blistering my thumb,
license plate patches keep out the rain.

"He" in a neat square, numbered, named—*Helium*—
balloon-swelling, evasive element.

The stairs past Boron, Silicon, Tellurium. Sad today,
the wood banister at my shoulder's solid, elemental.

Around us yucca flowers bloomed like hovering,
sweet moths, you understanding nothing: Lead.

Calcium's the clam, the exo- and the endoskeleton, oval
around the duck embryo, it defies the elements.

The thunder, I curl on my futon, on the floor
in the house, diminished by the elements.

"Cobalt" when I showed you evening over the road,
it was something more than blue that I meant.

❋ ❋ ❋

I bite into apple seeds for the almond taste,
cyanide, the bitter hint, liqueur trace.

An adolescent rabbit in the county dump, among cans,
bedsprings and other rusty oxidizing elements.

The garden's bordered with railroad ties, I weed
but things sucker out, the violets and mint.

Two Hydrogens, an Oxygen, some Chlorine—
me in it swimming, fish-like, elemental.

All shapes in a field: cluster of yarrow, cylindrical
trumpet vine, butterfly weed—crystalline.

I put words out—as if anything formed contains
any of the wishing, the days-to-days, the lake, dirt.

But you know this. The periodic table,
bread we eat, sleep, are all composed of elements.

The name they gave me, translated, innocuous flower.
Shortened, *winter*, season of finger-chilling days.

# Stories: Wolf Children

Dug out of the kettle-shaped
wolf den, Amala and Kamala
sleep in a monkey ball, lightly, one on top
the other. So many ways

to tell a story. The female wolf turning,
turning back, head lowered, ears
flat. Swift "Schwick"
of arrows, sleeping now

without her on the orphanage
floor.—Her warm flank
like the dog at the foot of my bed
when I was a girl—

Found by Reverend Singh, no—
brought to him by hunters; he
tells it twice, differently. Their eyes'
feral blue glow.

They crawl on all fours, steal
chicken entrails from the cook,
crouch in separate corners
their thin backs to the room only coming

together to nap. A decent frock
if they will ever stand.
Kamala steals a bone from the dogs, hides
it in the lantana's shadow.

The Bengal night, deep and low, before
they die of dysentery, first one
and then the other. They roam the cage,
cry "hoo, hoo,"
to everything we pretend to know.

# Stray Into, Away

Swirl of clothes leaching clean
    of bird lime, sunscreen. Neutral smell
of Fels Naptha in its paper wrapper,
    you remembered that longer than I
and reminded me once. Formaldehyde
    to preserve embryos, tern eggs
that never hatched. A medallion
    of sun glinting in the white basin.

We learned to drop the bucket into
    the cistern's bottomless sheen, upside down,
just right to catch the fill. Clang
    as it hits the iron bars, nylon rope
frayed, a row of complacent gerry cans
    to hold the icy water we funnel in.

The kestrel landing on the concrete sill
    at our faces, as we stood and stared
out to the sun and mobbing terns
    from the shade of the old bunker.
What we were saying is gone, we only
    meet occasionally, you still go back.
First miles of water, then the grey
    hazy stitch on the horizon, one boat
and all that room to stray in.

✳  ✳  ✳

After swimming, tired and numb from the tide
    coursing by, no bottom to touch
I'd haul out on the warm rocks, clean
    water lapping and the birds' calls faint,
head shrinking smaller than a pea stone,
    hovering. What was I doing, those days

spent hunched like a plastic turtle,
        in a blind of pipes and black tarp?

My great discoveries—a hollow
        lined with grass under a root, or on a pile
of crossed sticks—the hub the blunt-
        beaked sparrows had carried grubs to
for days, obvious now as peaches in a bowl,
        or a peregrine falcon—black speck
in a cloud of terns chasing it out to sea,
fireworks on the Connecticut shore,
        off Montauk, silent and untethered,
the night breeze on our faces. Things seemed
        to have no moorings. From the tower,
at dawn, the island like a piece of lath
        in the lead-colored water. One week
mustard blossoms, florescent yellow. Then green,
        then knobby seed pods. The sparrows
I watched eat grubs in the compost heap
        have rotted now, for sure, on the tide line
or dropped into the waves. Who's there?

� ✻ ✻ ✻

In and out of the abandoned tunnels, swallows
        chittering in the doorway, mud nests
built on the rusty gun hooks they've used
        for fifty, a hundred summers. Five
white-flecked eggs in the dark, the size
        of my finger pads. And all in one day,
loose skin and down, bills opening. Damp
        air, the parents all fussed-up,

iridescent. There are mornings I miss now
        if I wake early, pull on shorts and shirt,

walk out before the fog's off the streets —
    a river of stones in a front yard,
three-lobed cactus, a Brewer's Blackbird
    sighting a crumb under a café table — miss
cold air between ribs and arms, uncurling
    into the morning. You still go back,

waves of birds rise and settle
    as someone walks the length of the island.
My attempts, definitions, maps — the birds'
    territories numbered and circled,
the tagged sparrow singing from the same
    pile of rubble and bittersweet
three summers in a row. What I learned,

❈   ❈   ❈

at night, predators come — an owl, a heron
    with a cap and grey mantle. I've dreamed
of an owl clinging to my neck, white and black,
    in a bare room at the top of stairs.
Out there, the stars undiluted, distinct
    in the dark under the dark shell, thin pen-line
of a satellite. I've never wanted to write
    about writing, but I've tried this before —
my midden. Mussel shells, corncobs, lamb
    bones, the sparrows eating grubs
in the compost. Here's the kestrel, here's me
    walking away from something not finished.
The blackbird on the hill, recognizing
    my straw hat on someone else, swoops
from the tops of the honeysuckle,
    whirr and cuff on the tatty brim. *Rosa*

*rugosa*, nightshade, me not saying
 if I'll come back or not. What makes
a good end? Sometimes I think now
 there's none of this left in me, save
an urge to sleep late, rainy days. My maps,
 measurements of wings, lists of sparrows
each summer, a turnstone found dead
 on the north beach in fall, me thinking—
I'm like the army now, using a place and moving on.

# Mill Street

The fat woodchuck
learned to climb the fence
    around the vegetable garden
        and my mother
put the grandchildren to shaking
    the unsprayed tree

of winesaps,
onto the lawn, the stone wall,
    the chipped gravestone
        against the wall. They shook
and shook, cried "eat these, eat these,"
    but inevitably

rustles,
the woodchuck's wide back
    in among ripe tomatoes.
        The garden's frozen now,
dead stems and nubs. We go out—
    my niece and nephew,

Evie and Doug,
they want to know
    what the grown-over plow furrows are
        in the field.
In the late winter light, the gravemarker's
    easy to read,

the immense hull
of my brother's boat looks as if
    it wants to throw off its tarps,
        roll down to the river,
singing, "spring, spring!"
    we walk

the furrows,
bend to scramble under oak branches,
    slight space between cedars
        where deer have passed.
On the hill, the woodchuck
    who would not be fooled

    by green apples
has kicked gravel and sand
    out of its burrow, has this view
        of us, the boatyard,
marsh grass lying this way and that.
    The sun

    gone behind trees,
a flush on the ice, thin around pilings,
    cement boat slip,
        fish under mud.
We find a beer can washed up, broken pencil,
    a fishhook.

    Doug throws stones
onto the river, the frozen river
    that in spring they would drop into,
        disappear, but now
sounds the "whippet-whippet-whippet"
    of their spinning, holds.

# Letter Intercepted

After you left us, we stopped
combing our hair. You know
who we are, we followed
you from rock to rock, learned
to land only seconds
on the loose ones. Alpha dog,
leader. Our hair's matted
at our necks, on our tan arms
a white skim of a salt line.
We've spent days watching plovers
fly up with the foam, never talked
if you'd come back or not,
you were off—boat to bigger boat.
Some mornings we'd stand at the end
of the pier, open arms raised wide.
We know winter will come,
we found a dead bird in the sand,
fried its olive-sized liver
over the fire. Crouched,
we watched the black sticks and coals,
labels melting on the tin cans.

# My Shining Archipelago

A scattering of mottled seeds, spots
of the moon-and-stars melon. A cobalt sea
slips between cliffs and sand-
circled bays. Tug boats, a shadow
of a coasting gull.

❋ ❋ ❋

On Wona, the dead puppy's ghost
runs into my house, steals
butter from the kitchen table.

When he barks, his voice
is sweet and smooth, a singing drum.

❋ ❋ ❋

Last week on Luen, the island lecher
made a call, the telephone
became an orange is his hand,
a Seville orange. He has since
devoted his time (most diligently)
to tending the espaliered trees
growing against the garden wall.

❋ ❋ ❋

On Randherst, the gardeners
wear clogs, they step high and lose
them in the creeks. The shoes float,
painted skiffs, until the village collies
leap and fish them from the eddies.

❋ ❋ ❋

The general spends hours lobbing
softballs into the limbs
of the catalpa. There are four
schools, but none of them have gym
and this disturbs him. The catalpas
drop chocolate beans all over
the manicured lawns.

❋ ❋ ❋

The cows on the Winkapins
walk away from the stockyards
and into the fields, they eat
the purple blooming vetch
and watch each other with heavy-
lashed eyes. No one dares chase them.

❋ ❋ ❋

When it rains for days, the quarries
fill with fresh water. The shells
on the beaches stretch and shine.
Cotton grass, soft as hair on someone
you once touched, grows
into tassels of silk.

❋ ❋ ❋

When my plane catches fire
above the northern channel marker,
I'll forget to pull the exit
lever, pieces of wing will scatter,

the propeller split into blades
drifting down like maple seeds,
sand-circled, edged and cliffed.

# Four

✹ ✹ ✹

# Afterwards: Caliban

I learned to name them—brown-nut-warm, wide
Hipped, **horses,** on legs Thin as saplings.
They have smooth, knocking, beach-stone Hooves,
Are made to pull carriages, carry wood
Across London's dull paths. Ears like the hare
They speak a Soft Language. Sweet Breathers:
They exist solely on the Insubstantial
Grass, dusty Grains. The head is small—the size
Of an owl, a keg. I think once they owned
This island. In the warm ear of the one
That stops at The Bridge, I whisper: "wave"
"Oat cake," "the world is whip-less," "blue grey,"
I can see suns, a seed, clouds in its Eye,
From its Flank, it shivers off a sweat Fly.

✳   ✳   ✳

Its shit is sweet, Harmless, it crumbles
Under the Rain back into grass. I did
Fit in there, on the island, even after
**They** came. Here, housemaids throw refuse
Into the streets, Unclean city. The fresh
Springs still seeped cold, I knew the jays'
Call: the anis' "weep-weep"—how they Flew,
Shadow-birds, from reeds at the waves'
Edge when the boat came. I knew
Marmoset with Golden Paws, heavy-
Billed pelican, barnacle Goose-bird, dirt
Tunnel of the blind mole's home. We drank
The water; in small holes left our waste
And the bright Dung beetle rolled it away.

✳   ✳   ✳

Miranda, pig-nut, acorn, **space**—I now
Know what to call it, what surrounded us
When the island was still Sable from night—
The sea's Mercurial flush, endless dove grey,
The sky like water, but of Other
Colors: lavender to sand-yellow
Seamlessly—that it seemed I could Bathe in,
Like the Tortoise glides in the billows
On Armored wings. I did Feel this, standing
On the promontory; This he can not
Take from me; Deny I noticed the curl
Behind her ear. Curl, curly, **Curly Dock,**
The herbalist's poultice, heart's cure. Silly
Girl, sillier boy, who cares where they are now?

❊    ❊    ❊

Pears and rue, I walk the London physic
Garden. I knew they would Marry, they
Had the same Eyes; played Chess—I couldn't
Grudge them that. Squares of herbs, regiments
Of onions, parsley against a brick wall,
A wicker Cage for Doves. Why did I leave
The island? So many things I didn't know—
That I would be put out: Fleet Street, beside
The two-headed Infant found in the Thames;
The wicker ports; Garlic stink of People
Pressing close. They kept me until I picked
My scabs too much, slept, Dreamt. It's years ago.
Here: gillie-flower ("Nature's bastard," **carnation**)
Its warm, Breeze-borne scent: cinnamon.

❊    ❊    ❊

Evenings in Spring, the "chink-chinks" of Bells—
Morris Men dancing; and the Man-woman,
Who makes me nervous, his beard and House-wife's
Frock, is and isn't. The night also Strange.
Torches. There are Marvels in this city,
Houses Alight as if they've brought
The stars into their Bedchambers. Watching
Alone from a casement window the moon
Casts my lumped, ugly Shadow. Torch flames
Like salamanders, like the red Silk
In Cloaks. No, I never found Another
Like me. Alchemic Understanding—why
Does the Phoenix burn alone, others
In sympathy? I've known friends. Tyrants, too.

⁂ ⁂ ⁂

He would not carry wood himself, **Pros-
pero;** you are long since Dead but yet
You make me rage. His words and Spells; he
Played us like a Boy will a June bug
On a string—whirling it around his Head;
Like, by God's hand, the Sun orbiting
The Earth. The first Man I saw; the first Words
I heard, I listened to. I showed them ground
Nuts, ripe Fruits, the silver smooth, Blue mussel—
Inside, the Morsel of meat. I didn't
Hide the bog where the berries grew. He sucked
Out the bodies of Shrimps, then flogged me, bid
Me work, watched me, blisters and Bark; as if He
Knew the meaning, the Heft of leather, of wood.

⁂ ⁂ ⁂

I was his Pup, delight of his Eye
When first I looked to him, repeated: **moon, sun
sea**. It was Easy; I made my chants, caused
Her to laugh. Stood on wave-licked rocks, Able
To tell of my toe grip on the Kelp—what he
Had never Felt. He began to hide his books;
He cut my hand in front of Her. He taught me
**ugly**—before her; my reflection: gross
Head, mud-caked mouth . . . An openness in me
Collapsed. **Monster, monster;** he who knew my Joys
Did taunt me. I shoved him up to a Pine,
Twisted tight his cloak around his neck.
Yet he kicked my ribs, bent me; broke me. For nights
I slept, Folded; the pose of the Child.

❋   ❋   ❋

What does it matter if you can tell False
Visions, swell the air with your Words, make Tales
Intoxicate. What matters is what's here:
Spring veal and Peas, a warm bed, ale, the day
When you Wake, quarelling sparrows in the Eaves.
Or what's not here, my Island—is it still
There? A boat five Years ago couldn't See
Its Bluffs. Perhaps eaten? Prospero ate
All the Mussels from the rocks where the Plover
Slept; perhaps Sunk under the Waves. When I
Think of it, it's in Days before they came,
When ginger root still bloomed at the cave.
It's the past, in my Head, Pictures: the bright
Metal brought from the Stone called Memory.

❋   ❋   ❋

And yet, **words.** Because I could speak I lived
As scullion and Gardener to Lord North's cook.
Fetched cherries, carrots, cabbages and Fish;
Turned the spit of Beef at the fire
When Shep the Terrier escaped. We grew
The new found Virginia potato.
Knobbly as my hands, dirt brown; in Spring
They'd sprout long pale Fingers in their dark Box.
Unremarkable, ugly, I'd chop
Them into Pieces, drop them in the Earth
Where they'd grow various. The King's ships
Brought them from the land where the Mountain turf
Hides gold. A plant like Snuff makes Lips
Grow numb; potatoes' skins are royal Blue.

❋   ❋   ❋


The Tulip, too, was in those days a novelty—
Ruffle-edged, flared, flamed, with names
Of Dukes and Duchesses, Queens—all from an
Onion-like Bulb. My days were ordered Rows
Of leeks: wake, eat, tidy and weed, harvest.
Into portions, **He** first, divided my days—as if
I didn't know to Wake: wood-time, dig-time,
**Piss**-time. Schedule and Rules, farewell sleeping
Until the need to wake. Before my Dreams
Were spent he made me rise, pull Dill seed
Before it dried. Not everything can come
From Books, lines of ink-grid numbers; I place
Carnations in the earth, they break Forth
Mysterious in Spring: some here, Red; there, Striped.

❋   ❋   ❋

In the Tower, on thin straw, they keep Lions.
Any street Boy or Fish-monger can watch
Them eat, sleep, Mate. What was once wondrous
Will no longer be—a Galileo
Has invented **telescope,** with which
One can see the World, falcon-like; can count
The stars: Leo; Capricorn, the goat,
Whose Humour is phlegmatic; the Moon—
They will peer at its Man, its light, order
It remain one-sized. The serpent that Crushes
Ships is still a mystery, and none I know
Have seen the Bishop fish but in pictures.
Herbalists keep plants' Portraits, incorporeal;
Flattened, they possess no Scents.

※   ※   ※

The boxwoods loom in the Dusk: dark
Beasts, elephants, a triangular monster,
Forgetful ostrich. Under my foot the shells
On the Path shift and crunch. So much one says
Like Seed, does not come True. Should I say **island?**
The Cook, squeezing a green Cabbage worm, would not
See **that** Bay, that particular promon-
tory. Talk, His barren talk, and Oaths. It seems
My island grows smaller, not Fixed
In Rhumb-lines on any Map. The Reare-mice
On leather wings, the Hedges, dissolve into
Night. My cane-taps sound far away.
What I tell you, what I tell you—
It is so much smaller than what I can not tell you.